The ABC's of Appreciation
Let your heart speak

Published by Katja Rossel

1st print edition January 2019

Inquiries should be addressed to:
Katja Rossel
www.katjarossel.info
mail@katjarossel.info

3

To Laslo, Yannick and Robert

Many thanks ...

... to my trainers, coaches and friends, who taught me these tools the past 15 years and kept reminding me to improve. They also helped me with this book. You are great!

Table of Contents

Acknowledgement...8
Belief...10
Connection...12
Distinctions...14
Environment...16
Feedback..18
Genius..20
High Energy...22
Interest..24
Just say Yes..26
Kindness..28
Laughter..30
Mood..32
Not Personal..34
Observation...36
Playfulness..38
Questions...40
Respect..42
Storytelling...44
To be in service...46
Unity...48
Voice..50
What works..52
X - times..54
Yielding..56
Zen..58

Introduction

The importance of appreciation became clear to me when I was nineteen years old. I did an apprenticeship as a clerk in a pharmaceutical company in Berlin. I watched as the leader of the packing department enthusiastically mentioned an idea to the CEO, who was passing by. The CEO's only reply was: "You should not think. You should just work." She left the woman and me feeling humiliated. At that moment, I decided I would not continue working at this company after my apprenticeship. I decided to embark on a search for how to encounter people in an appreciative way.

On this journey, I came across the many aspects of appreciative communication which I'd like to share with you. It changed my view and my life for the better. I hope it also changes your perspective and your life for the better, too.

Acknowledgement

Put your focus on what works. Acknowledge yourself and others five or more times a day. Be specific. Name activities and actions. Keep a list of the acknowledgements you make to yourself. Be sure to notice when your acknowledgement reaches out and brings a smile to people's faces.

Sandra worked as a pharmacist on a great team. The payment was modest compared to what colleagues earned in other institutions, but no one on that team ever had any desire to leave. For years, the team worked together. Their boss had an incredibly benevolent nature. Sandra and her colleagues valued him highly. All were delighted to work. Special requests for working hours, free time or special scheduling was met with few exceptions and without any bureaucracy. Sandra felt the trust of the supervisor in her and her colleagues. In the course of restructuring, the boss was transferred and new working hours were installed. The wages increased. Sandra and her colleagues were very pleased to earn more. Nevertheless, after a short period of time, Sandra no longer felt acknowledged. Working conditions deteriorated drastically. Personal wishes were only considered through a large bureaucratic approach. The new supervisor wanted to do the right thing, but wasn't a bit warm and not at all sympathetic. Sandra and her team all began to consider leaving their jobs.

elief

Believe in people. It is amazing what you can achieve if there is a person who is very sure you can make it. It is this deep trust that assists us to really go for it.

You might start with believing that you have great children who will be wonderful and sweet people as adults. People can grow and succeed if there is at least one person who believes in them. Be one of those who create outstanding and great people. Begin to believe in everyone around you. Just try this for one week and you will be astonished by what happens. You will begin to attract like-minded people who start believing in you and your greatness. And guess what? It will be easier to reach outstanding results and feel great.

(Remember: It also works the other way around. If you think everybody is an idiot, you will be surrounded by those.....)

Ben, an engineer, wrote a book on communication between men and women. This is a topic he researched for a couple of years by attending communication classes and observing reality. His greatest fan is his mother. She accompanies him to all his book readings, sells the books when he is talking to guests, and just believes in him. She not only speaks her belief, she demonstrates it!

He often says this is what made going on the adventure of being an author possible.

onnection

Feeling connected is a great feeling. It is the basis of good communication. The moment you meet someone, two different people get together: two different upbringings, two different ways of seeing the world, two different opinions about almost everything. Develop your curiosity about this other person. Have a closer look, and put your assumptions away. Your deep curiosity will help a person to open up and share. If you learn to restore your curiosity you won't have boring conversations anymore, and you will enjoy the feeling of deep connections.

Be interested and open. Follow the curiosity of the other person by asking questions.

Maria and Nicole write a book together. They collect interviews with people on the topic of work. To finish the book, and find a common way of writing and working on the book, they really need a good connection. Both keep in contact on a regular basis. They write each other text messages, e-mails or leave messages on the phone almost every day. They also are very curious about each other and talk often about their individual goals, in general and concerning the book. They also share their ideas and perspectives and stay interested in each other.

$\mathcal{D}$istinctions

Start making distinctions. Have a look and see whether you are tired or excited, curious or bored, animated or still. Please have a look at the people around you as well. What kind of activities light people up? What kinds of activities make them alive, curious and happy? Watch people and look for when they light up. When talking about certain subjects, people will either have bright eyes or not. Be aware of the changes in people and the differences in their behavior, posture and presence. Yield to the changes. In conversations, follow the topics where people get animated. This will bring a lot of joy into your life and into the lives of the people you are talking to.

Today, observe two people and notice how the appearance of their eyes changes during a conversation.

Sonya likes to get up early in the morning. She is full of energy when she starts the day. She realized that her energy drops in the evening and that she has a hard time answering e-mails and working on her business. She observed herself for several months and discovered her personal rhythm. She stopped making appointments late in the day and instead only does routine work then. For Valerie, her business partner, it is the other way around. She sleeps long and can't keep a thought together in the morning. So they learned not to make their joint meetings too early or too late in the day.

nvironment

This is about what surrounds you. The environment has a great impact on us. We may feel welcome and appreciated when we step into a room, or scared and aggressive. We feel the atmosphere. When a party is going on you feel the lightness, enjoyment, and fun. In a room where people are debating you feel the heaviness, maybe even the fighting and rudeness in the "air".

As we are able to observe this, we are able to create an atmosphere as well. What kind of environment makes you happy and light? Be sure to be there as often as you can!

Make a list of five aspects of environment that make you happy and light.

Julian is 5 years old and loves to play with ALL his toys. He empties everything in his closet and boxes onto the floor. For a few days he sits happy in the middle of this big mess. Then suddenly he has a hard time playing. He starts to take his toys out of his room and play in the hallway or other rooms. His parents realize that they need to help Julian get back into a clear space in his room to start the cycle all over again.

Feedback

Say what you see. Don't give advice or criticize or interpret other people's behavior and words. Speak just what you see as precisely and concretely as possible. Refrain from any accusations.

Give feedback twice tomorrow.

For example:

- "Wow, you are charming!"
- "Thank you for handing me my jacket."
- "You can really scream!"

July's husband was good with numbers and helped her in her business. He did the accounting and the taxes. One day she came home late after a meeting with a client. Her husband ran to her and shouted: "Your paperwork is a mess. You never give me the papers on time." A flood of accusations rolled down the hallway. She felt attacked and wrong and was almost going to defend herself. She realized that this was all about his concern and anxiety over turning in the numbers late to the tax authorities. So she simply asked: "Are you afraid that we will be late?" He paused. His faced relaxed and he said in a normal voice: "Yes, you are right, I want to turn in everything on time". The fight ended before it really started and they got back to work to meet the due date.

Genius

What is your genius, and how do you recognize the genius in others? Each of us carries a special talent: a dedication to a theme or an activity, a gift. Be curious about what it could be for you and for others.

Usually, well hidden from the rest of the world, we think, "I am nothing. I can do nothing. I hope nobody notices." You can break this habit by finding out what you are brilliant in. We are gifted with what can seem to be nothing really special. It seems normal to us and something anyone could do. But there you can find your talent.

As you start trusting your talents, it is easier to see the brilliance in others. Enjoy your gifts so that you can enjoy others' gifts as well.

This way you begin to see people from an appreciative point of view.

Ask your friends what they see as your genius and tell them how you see theirs.

Robert and Mandy bought a new house. It had to be renovated. Old wallpaper had to be taken down, but there were many pieces which would not come off. You had to scratch little pieces off the wall either with your nail or a small knife. Both of them hated to do this job. When they spoke of the task with their friend Michael, his genius, gift and talent for this came to shine. It turned out he liked it. He enjoyed working slowly and precisely, with great care. He would not have been right for the heavier tasks requiring strength. This task was perfect for him. He lit up on it and was a big help.

 igh Energy

Be enthusiastic. You transmit high energy when you do what you love to do. This is more than communication. This is dedicating your life to enthusiasm and ease. With high energy you move people and money. In technology, we would talk about high-end technical products. For your communication, "high energy" is a high-end tool. The vibration you are sending out is about 90 percent of your communication. You actually move people with your energy, low and high. Words and gestures make up only about 10 %.

So, keep your vibes high.

Do at least one activity you are enthusiastic about each day for a week.

Thomas published a book on short stories. Three of his female friends loved his way of writing and promised to set up a reading session in their town. They were so enthusiastic about this project that they told everybody about it. They even decided to meet for a session with a photographer to have pictures taken. They titled the series "3 Angels for Thomas". It was so much fun. When they posted their pictures on Facebook, people told them they could feel the fun and enthusiasm simply by looking at the pictures.

nterest

We are naturally curious and interested. As children, we look at the world with bright eyes and full of wonder. Growing up, we lose our curiosity and this bright outlook. We are filled with knowledge. As adults we are mostly concerned about what will be. We worry.

Start asking yourself: "What does my heart really want?", and start actively following this path. The expression of your eyes will change. They will be clearer and more radiant.

Now you can look around and watch when other people's eyes get brighter. Notice too when their voice is more animated, when they look clearer, and when their skin has more color, as both their body and face relaxes.

Start lighting up. Listen to the aliveness and glow.

Ask two friends what they love doing and watch to see if their eyes turn bright.

Claire and Yvonne have a great conversation. Claire was a guest at an "Open Stage Show", where the audience is invited to go onstage and be part of the show, and she liked it very much. She had fun watching and being a part of this fun crowd. When Yvonne suggested she jump on stage herself the next time she answered, "No, this is not for me at all. I just like the atmosphere at this event". Nevertheless, Yvonne watched her closely and saw that Claire was lighting up, smiling, and that her eyes turned bright when she talked about being on stage. Yvonne did not just listen to Claire's words, but rather her body talk, and stayed interested.

Just say Yes

Start building an attitude of "just say yes". Be the catalyst for relaxed interactions. The opposite is "yes, but". This blocks the flow. "Just say yes" opens the door for good energy to flow, especially in teams.

With the next person you meet, think: "Yes, right on!"

Gwen and Jennifer plan to travel to Paris together. They both love the city. They don't know each other that well yet, but they like each other's company and both love to travel. What works well is that they are both very eager to come up with ideas of what to see and do during their stay. This makes the planning easy. Even though a lot of what they planned did not work out - closed museums, very small hotel room, etc. - they both kept the attitude of "just say yes" and had a great trip.

Kindness

With kindness, you open your heart and open the door to other people's hearts.

To communicate appreciatively you need to have an open heart. This is what we were like as kids. As we grew older we heard comments which hurt us, people said things which turned down our lights, and we had experiences which made us close our hearts. Otherwise we could not bear the pain.

Now, when you open your heart, all this pain and suffering can come up again. Give in and cry. With time the pain will wane and you can keep your heart open. This will lead to encounters of mutual goodwill and appreciation in every arena of your life.

Of course, you will continue to meet people who attack and hurt you, unconsciously and consciously. Learn to defend yourself against the "Dark Arts". This is more about observing and rerouting than fighting and defending yourself. It is a sophisticated art which is worth learning. It is about Feedback, Laughter, Observation and Zen.

Look at your environment with a warm, kind view.

In this respect my favorite example is Nelson Mandela. He was imprisoned for over 20 years. He kept his dignity and his kindness throughout this awful long period of time. If he can do it, we can do it at least once in a while.

Laughter

Be full of laughter. Don't take everything so seriously. Decide to have a humorous outlook. The world will appear friendlier. Make jokes, play games and be at ease. Go along with things. If you are not so funny, just smile and spread your lightness.

Laugh out loud five times today.

Dan works as a gardener for a family who owns a mansion surrounded by a park. He is getting old, but he loves his work. When he is in pain, his wife has a great way of transforming his bad mood. She talks to him in a warm voice, calls him "an old man", and puts him to bed like a child, with a big grin on her face. He always starts to smile and giggle. Even though the words and scenario do not change, it makes him laugh.

Mood

We all have certain moods throughout the day. We feel happy, enthusiastic, alone, anxious, sad, in self-pity, angry. Please don't instill your bad mood on other people without asking. Bad moods are like viruses. They spread quickly and pull everybody else into the same mood you are in. And then you feel worse!

Look for a place to put it. Do you need professional help to deal with life's challenges? Can you go for a walk to let it settle?

Activities change your mood for the better most of the time. You can either get active with something you like doing, or put your mood into what you do. Pour your bad mood - anger, sadness, anxiety - into cleaning the bathroom. This way you don't inflict it on other people. You will harvest what you nourish, in any case.

Spread your good mood and greet everyone enthusiastically.

Fred decided not to inflict his bad mood on his wife and his kids. When he comes home pressured and full of anger, he puts on his running shoes and goes jogging.

For Lucy, the world is sometimes really an awful place. Nothing is the way it should be. She then decides to call a friend for a minute of whining. She makes sure this is in an entertaining way. Her friend always laughs and Lucy feels lighter.

Daniel chooses to sit down every morning and write what he dislikes and everything that gets on his nerves. After collecting these thoughts, he throws the paper in the trash can.

ot Personal

You are always right. Everyone else is always right. Keep this in mind and don't take anything personally. People are so busy with their lives, just like you. We easily project our feelings and thoughts onto others.

Instead, step aside with the attitude "this has nothing to do with me". Sometimes we expect certain outcomes or certain reactions. This is what you have on your mind. You don't have a clue what somebody else has on their mind. You do what you do. Other people do what they do. The skill of observation helps to not take anything personally.

Just watch what appears in front of you.

Every game has its rules. During the game the players need to stick to the rules. If they break the rules, they have to deal with the consequences. Sometimes players take this personally, but not for the rest of their lives. It's just the rules. It's not personal.

To make it into the 100-yard relay, runners have to try out, and the best make it. The results determine the choice. It is not personal and nobody should take it personally.

bservation

Look around. Look around with all your senses. Listen to the noise around you. Feel the atmosphere in the room you are in. Does it smell good or bad?

It is really interesting to see what's there. Do not interpret. Leave your opinions alone. Put your attitudes aside. Nobody argues with nature. The sky is blue, trees are green and the sun is bright.

Look at five people as if they were a painting, what do you see?

Andy, a building engineer, had a supervisor who yelled in every meeting and was in a rage. Regularly, Andy was confronted with his anger and disapproval. Andy had no problem leading his projects, nor did the projects go badly. Nevertheless, he found the tantrums to be unbearable. It was his third position within the last 2 years where he had to cope with aggressive supervisors. Then he had the idea to just watch the actions of his boss and not to take it personally. At first he observed that there were times of madness and times of friendliness. Andy also started to see the act as a play in a theatre. The pressure started to lift off him, and within some weeks the supervisor stopped acting so mad when he was in close contact with Andy. Their cooperation became much easier.

Playfulness

Playfulness is a great tool to make life exciting. By creating fun games you enjoy the day better; life appears lighter and so will your communication. It is all about creating games with yourself and other people. Fun games could be:

- Acknowledge 10 people today

- Lower the stress by 3 points on a scale from 1 to 10

- Throw a "cleaning party" with your kids

- Do 10 important tasks before drinking a nice hot chocolate with whipped cream

- Do homework for school with a friend

What game will you play tomorrow?

Anne lived alone with her 2 sons for the last 7 months. Her husband was working abroad. How could she find a way to get everything done, which was usually split between the two? She decided to set up "cleaning parties" at home. She bought snacks and sweets and made a list of all the tasks. The kids liked the idea and chose what they had fun doing. Anne's aim was to have fun as well and get more done than if she had been alone. They turned on the music and started. The 5 year old stopped cleaning after the fourth task was done, but at the same time, 4 tasks were finished. His big brother kept his excitement a little bit longer. At the same time, Anne kept her good mood throughout the day, and more was done altogether.

${\mathcal{Q}}$uestions

It is all about not-knowing. People are very interesting when you approach them with this attitude, this curiosity. Go ahead and keep your attitudes, opinions, ideas, and knowledge about the world, people in general, and yourself. But once in a while, put them aside and perceive yourself and others as a great wonder.

Asking questions is the tool for that. Don't tell what you know. Instead, ask, "How do you feel?", "What would it be like to...", "How do you take in the world?" Asking open-ended questions is the best way to invite people to talk and share. The more you let them be the way they are, the more they will share what's really important and what they really want.

Small kids ask hundreds of questions. They are very curious. Restore that habit.

Respect

Everything is alright, everything is fine. Whatever people do, it is fine the way they do it. We cannot do anything about it anyway. With a respectful attitude you touch people's hearts. They won't feel wrong. We all long to be deeply respected the way we are. You don't have to agree, but respect.

Write 3 things about what you respect in your partner, your child, and your colleagues.

The 8th grade Spanish teacher had big problems with the kids. She could not inspire them to engage during the lessons. She lost the ability to lead this group more and more. She yelled and screamed constantly at the kids in an inappropriate way. The parents wanted a meeting and went armed for battle. Luckily, one mother reminded everyone to behave respectfully. The parents and their children want to be treated with respect. This should also apply to the teacher.

Storytelling

Tell inspiring stories. Share what worked in your life. It is better to inspire by telling a story than giving advice. Nobody really wants to hear that. Share stories which make you love and laugh. People will enjoy that and everybody will learn. Shared experiences enrich our lives. Tell stories of what you plan to do and what you dream of doing and having. Brainstorm how your plans and dreams may be realized. Share stories on that.

Share two inspiring stories with two different people tomorrow.

Jennifer has been married for 18 years. Since she met her husband she has never spread a bad word about him. He certainly is not perfect, but nobody needs to know. She will not badmouth him.

$\mathcal{T}$o be in service

To master a service attitude will certainly serve you. In a service economy you will be paid for being friendly, sincere and sweet. No one wants to be treated by a grumpy massage therapist, buy a computer and feel stupid, or take a painting class and feel awkward. People who serve other people well will make good money.

Imagine what your service could be to the world. By smiling at others, you will enrich other people's lives. By listening carefully and being interested, you give your attention. By being interested in other people's well-being, you will be in service.

Take their perspective and see what they need. Put your own needs aside for a moment.

Within the next 5 days help a friend to get closer to their goal.

Wendy attended a business coach's training and was very impressed. She followed his instructions and turned out to be happier and moved more money. Now she wanted to give something back and help him. She signed up to assist his company.

She was on the team of the manager on duty who gave her one task after the other. "Amazingly", she told her best friend Tina later that day: "I started to feel more free during the day, just being responsible for a single task at a time." She was amazed that she felt inspired and at ease by the end of the day.

nity

Together is always easier than alone. How can you come to a win-win situation and feel united? How do you get what you need to be happy? How can you help others to be happy? Often we assume it is a virtue to get everything handled alone.

Forget this way of thinking. Look to see how you can help others reach their goals. Find those who are willing and will have fun helping you reach your goals.

This attitude creates a feeling of unity and brings people together. People relax and feel secure and appreciated.

Ask a person for help.

Peter wanted to create a big fashion show. He was a small business owner with the ability to win people over to help him. For the fashion show he needed models, so he set up a model casting call. Four hundred girls and boys applied to be a part of this event for free.

Fashion designers made up the jury to find models who would show their collections.

Photographers were also asked to take pictures during the casting for free. They had a chance to meet a lot of people who would love to have pictures taken and book a photography session.

Coaches held complimentary workshops to meet new clients and get films and pictures for marketing. All together they were able to present a great event.

Voice

The tone of your voice transports your actual mood, vibration and presence. You are able to change your mood. If you open your heart to someone your voice will immediately be warmer and deeper. You can start by faking your mood, as it might not be sweet in the beginning. You just make your voice warm and deep. Your mood will change due to that in the long run.

Speak with a warm heart today to at least one person.

Katie and Gwen talk about their jobs and exchange the latest news. Both of them really want to share what is going on in their lives and what they are up to. Nevertheless, Katie feels Gwen's anxiety and tightness, so she changes her tone of voice, puts her whole heart in it and says, "You are quite challenged at the moment, right?" Gwen starts to cry and her pain comes to the surface. Just this change of voice allows her to drop her mask and relax.

 hat works

All day long you do a lot of things that work. You earn money, care about your kids, answer the questions of your fellow co-workers, and wash the dishes and a lot more.

Please put your attention on what works and not on what does not work. Each day write down 5 things you did that worked. Your mood will change for the better, and you will begin to attract different, more positive people into your life.

Tonight, write 5 actions that worked during the day.

Lisa could not point out what works. Nothing she did was special; she just did what she had to do. By taking a look at what works and writing this down, her presence and her view on life changed for the better.

A few months after she started doing this, her friends say that she has changed. She seems more positive and it's fun to be around her. Her classes are full now and the participants have started bringing their friends.

 - times

You will need to say an acknowledgement several times before you make a request. Generally, with women you need to say 8 acknowledgements before making a request. With men, it is twice as many.

Point out to people what they've done many times. Use observation and your attention to see when people smile, talk enthusiastically, come in on time, write e-mails and so on. There are hundreds of details we do and we love to be acknowledged for them.

Acknowledge one person 8 times for 8 different activities or results.

The last time Martin asked for a raise and explained all the reasons he should get it, his previous supervisor did not react positively, nor did he get his raise. This time, he wants to do it differently. He considered what he could acknowledge her for. What did she do? During their conversation he mentions several aspects of her work he appreciates. She becomes more receptive, and this time he sits in front of someone who turns out to be willing and open to help him with his goal.

Yielding

Yielding is the fine art of knowing when to give in and when to push. Stop fighting for your point of view. It is right and the other point of view is right as well. Stop cramping your belly; just relax and exhale.

Make other people right. You don't need to give up your point of view. It's like yielding in traffic: you stop, let the cars pass by, and continue your journey a little bit later. You wait for the right moment. This way you can lead. This way everybody reaches their goal.

Today, disagree with no one. Pause and just listen.

It is Sunday evening. Betsy and her husband, Roland, are at home. She has a nice evening sitting outside on the porch on her mind. But Roland turns on the TV. His favorite show just starts. Betsy starts to be angry: "This is not how I expected the evening to be." Her frustration takes over every cell in her body. Then she pauses for a second. "What do I want?" she asks herself. "Well, to have a nice evening. What can I do to have a nice evening?" She keeps thinking and remembers her internet research project. Enthusiastically, she turns on her computer and realizes that she calms down and her fun rises. Suddenly her husband stands in the doorway. He's turned off the TV and now watches what she does curiously. Betsy suggests going outside to enjoy the summer breeze. They step outside....

en

Zen is about Contemplation, a great tool to get into a happy and calm state. Starting with this, you can't be anything other than appreciative. You do this by grounding yourself, connecting to the world, connecting with God, letting go.

You may do this through meditation, walking, jogging, reading books, sitting by the fireplace, taking a deep breath, exhaling, etc.

In contemplation, you find yourself. And you become calm, sweet and appreciative.

Now breathe in and out three times.

When I rush from one appointment to another, rush to day care to pick up the kids and rush to a meeting in the evening, I notice I am not in contemplation. Interestingly, life seems to be more of a struggle every day and the money flows less easily.

When I wake up and see the pressure I created for myself - I stop. It's time to stop, to slow down and contemplate. Often I schedule my day so that I have at least 30 minutes by myself.

For some people contemplation is to remember and bring up pictures of wonderful moments in their life, to do yoga, meditate, walk or jog.

For me, it is to sit in a café and read a magazine full of beautiful people and have a hot chocolate. It works every time. My breath deepens, my brain gets clear, and tranquility spreads in my body. "Things" seem to arrange themselves around me. Clients call for coaching, companies finally set dates for trainings, co-workers reschedule so that it fits me better, I am more in contact with what I want, and I am more able to enjoy my highly energetic kids.

Epilogue

Thank you for taking your time to read these suggestions. You probably realize that there are repetitions. The individual aspects of an appreciative communication intertwine and complement each other. Start with one of the 26 aspects and master it. You will be amazed how fast situations and people change for the better.

At the same time, know that you will not be perfect in appreciative communication immediately. This is not what you should aim for. Just give your best. It's worth it.

If you are eager to communicate appreciatively, please share this with your friends. If you like, you may host a book reading or an "evening of appreciation" by contacting me at mail@katjarossel.info. I love to connect with new people all over the world, via Skype and in-person. Also, please share your stories and experiences. I would love to publish them on my website www.katjarossel.info. What situations have you encountered? With which tool did you start?